All-New
Allstar Hockey
Activity Book

For
**Rolf
Maurer**

All-New
Allstar Hockey
Activity Book

Noah Ross & Julian Ross

POLESTAR
BOOK PUBLISHERS

Published by:
Polestar Press Ltd.
Gr. 12, C.9, R.R. #1
Winlaw, BC, Canada, V0G 2J0
and
2758 Charles Street
Vancouver, BC, Canada, V5K 3A7

Cover design by Jim Brennan
Cover photos by Chris Relke
Interior photos by Chris Relke and Bob Mummery
Illustrations by Anne DeGrace
Production by Julian Ross and Michelle Benjamin
Printed in Canada on recycled paper by Best-Gagne

**The authors would like to thank
Jesse Ross and Ruth Porter
for all their help.**

Canadian Cataloguing in Publication Data

Ross, Noah, 1982-
The all new allstar hockey activity book
ISBN 0-919591-89-2
1. National Hockey League—Miscellanea.
2. Hockey players—Miscellanea. I. Ross, Julian, 1952-
II. DeGrace, Anne. III. Title.
IV. Title: Allstar hockey activity book.
GV847.25.R68 1993   j.796.962'64   C93-091689-1

Use a pencil for the quizzes and puzzles—you'll be able to do them
again, or challenge a friend, parent, sister or brother.

CONTENTS

NICKNAMES

You probably know who Grapes and The Great One are, but can you figure out all of these nicknames?

Match the players' real names with their nicknames.

Pavel Bure	House
Stu Grimson	Captain Kirk
Bobby Hull	Russian Rocket
Brett Hull	Alexander The Great
Al Iafrate	Golden Brett
Darius Kasparaitis	Finnish Flash
Ted Kennedy	The Next One
Mario Lemieux	Chicoutimi Cucumber
Eric Lindros	Golden Jet
Kirk McLean	Teeder
Alexander Mogilny	Super Mario
Mark Recchi	Lethal Lithuanian
Vladimir Ruzicka	Pukie
Jim Sandlak	Trots
Teemu Selanne	Rosie
Bryan Trottier	Gump
George Vezina	Double Z
Lorne Worsley	Wild Thing
Zarley Zalapski	Rex
Valeri Zelepukin	Grim Reaper

WHERE WERE THEY BORN?

In 1973, only North American players were picked in the NHL draft. In the 1993 draft, 91 international players were chosen out of a total of 286. The NHL is truly becoming an international league. In the last few years, there have even been players drafted from such unlikely hockey hotbeds as the Bahamas and Japan.

Still, more Canadian players were chosen in the 1993 draft than any other nationality, with a total of 137; the United States was second with 55; Russia was third with 25; Sweden had 16; Czech Republic had 13; Finland had 8; and Ukraine had 5.

Match these players with the country in which they were born.

Pavel Bure—*Canucks/RW*	Scotland
Doug Gilmour—*Maple Leafs/C*	Russia
Brian Glynn—*Oilers/D*	Czechoslovakia
Mark Hardy—*Kings/D*	Northern Ireland
Jaromir Jagr—*Penguins/RW*	Sweden
Brian Leetch—*Rangers/D*	South Korea
Jyrki Lumme—*Canucks/D*	Germany
Owen Nolan—*Nordiques/RW*	Canada
Jim Paek— *Penguins/D*	United States
Steve Smith—*Blackhawks/D*	Switzerland
Mats Sundin—*Nordiques/C*	Finland

 Canada

 Sweden

 Switzerland

 South Korea

ARE YOU KIDDING?

1 Defenseman Lee Norwood broke his ankle midway through the 1992-'93 season when:
☑ his motorcycle fell on him.
☐ he fell down after celebrating a goal.
☐ he blocked an Al Iafrate slapshot.

2 Which NHLer pitched for Team Canada in the Little League World Series?
☑ Ray Ferraro
☐ Wayne Gretzky
☐ Kirk Muller

3 Which NHLer played in the Canadian Professional Soccer League?
☐ Gino Cavallini
☐ Luciano Borsato
☑ Peter Zezel

4 Craig Ludwig was sidelined with a sprained neck late in the 1992-'93 season when he was:
☐ cross-checked by Gino Odjick.
☐ wrestling with his kids on a day off.
☑ hit in the face with a whipped-cream pie, thrown by his teammates on his birthday.

5 In the 1992-'93 Stanley Cup finals, which player scored one goal and assisted on three others for his own team—plus scored the other team's goal—in a 4 - 1 win?

❑ Kelly Hrudey
☑ Wayne Gretzky
❑ Kirk Muller

6 What player almost led the league in penalty minutes two years in a row, then went on to twice win the Lady Byng (the trophy for clean play and skill)?

☑ Tiger Williams
❑ Stan Mikita
❑ Pierre Turgeon

7 The NHL recently attempted to introduce more Americans to hockey by:

☑ having the Kings play an exhibition game against the Rangers in a Las Vegas hotel parking lot.
❑ holding an NHL Skills Competition on portable ice during halftime at the Super Bowl.
❑ having a contest in which the winners get ten shots on the NHL goalie of their choice.

CONCENTRATION

Sticking Your Tongue Out Is A Good Thing?

Seriously—have you noticed that action photos of athletes sometimes show them with their tongues sticking out? You would think it's a pretty dumb thing to do, especially while playing hockey. But don't laugh. Scientists call it "tongue showing," and it's actually quite common. Without realizing what they are doing, people often stick their tongue out a little bit when they are concentrating deeply. Scientists say it sends a "stay away from me" message to others. You probably even do it yourself when you are really focussing.

Once we became aware of it, we started to realize how common it is. It's also a cross-nationality thing. We've found Russians, Czechs, Canadians, Americans, Finns and Swedes in our cards—all showing their tongues. Following is a list of some of the players we found, and their card numbers. You might want to check and see if you have any of the players listed below, or find examples of your own in your own card collection.

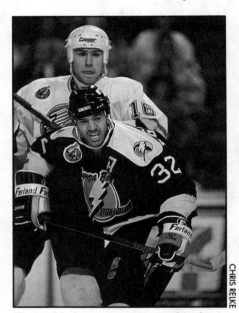

Trevor Linden concentrates on his check.

Dimitri Khristich (#16R, OPC '90)
Gary Roberts (#22, Parkhurst '93)
Roman Hamrlik (Premier #2, OPC '93)
Allen Pedersen (#300, Parkhurst '93)
Mike Hartman (#407, Parkhurst '93)
Bob Sweeney (#198, Upper Deck '91)
Scott Young (#87, Upper Deck '91)
Chris Chelios (#278, ProSet '91)

Joe Murphy (#68, ProSet '91)
Rob Blake (#302, Parkhurst '93)
Geoff Courtnall (#150, Score '91)
Joe Sakic (#199, ProSet '91)
Ray Ferraro (#156, ProSet '91)
Brian Propp (#2, Upper Deck '91)
Phil Bourque (#189, ProSet '91)
Ulf Samuelsson (#82, Score '91)

FAN FAVOURITES

We've hidden the last names of these current fan favourites in the word-search puzzle below. Their names are written either forwards or backwards, and placed horizontally, vertically or diagonally. The left-over letters (26 of them), taken in order from top to bottom, spell out the last names of four of hockey's greatest players of the past.

```
S  L  A  J  E  T  N  O  M  A
F  E  A  L  Y  R  U  E  L  F
E  G  L  U  R  A  H  R  O  W
R  I  S  A  E  R  R  U  I  C
R  L  E  H  N  D  Y  B  A  S
E  M  T  J  U  N  E  A  U  O
I  O  A  R  L  O  E  D  E  R
S  U  O  I  T  B  H  S  P  D
S  R  G  T  O  S  I  U  T  N
E  O  O  C  I  K  A  S  L  I
M  O  Y  K  Z  T  E  R  G  L
```

Tony AMONTE	Doug GILMOUR	Joe JUNEAU	Adam OATES
Peter BONDRA	Wayne GRETZKY	Eric LINDROS	Joel OTTO
Pavel BURE	Brett HULL	Mark MESSIER	Joe SAKIC
Theoren FLEURY	Jaromir JAGR	Alexander MOGILNY	Teemu SELANNE

_ _ _ _ _ _ _ ★ _ _ _ _ ★ _ _ _ _ _ _ ★ _ _ _ _ _ _ _

SPORTS PHOTOGRAPHERS

Most hockey clubs have their own team photographer who takes pictures for club programs, yearbooks, and advertising. As well, many professional and freelance photographers cover the NHL for newspapers and magazines. They also hope to get some great individual player shots that they'll be able to sell to card companies or poster makers.

But shooting game-action photos is a hard business that takes patience and perseverance. Some photographers shoot up to 300 pictures per game, and get only a few usable shots. They—like everyone else watching—never know when a game-winning goal or game-turning hit is about to happen.

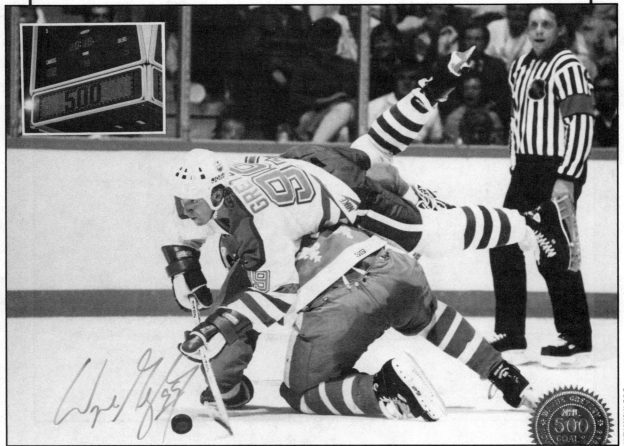

BOB MUMMERY

Photographers mostly sit in the front row at games. When you've been watching a game on TV, have you noticed their telephoto lenses sticking through holes in the plexiglass, usually between the face-off circle and goal? Some even have their cameras hooked up to expensive strobe flashes mounted in the catwalks high above the ice surface; when they take a picture, the above-ice flash automatically goes off, giving them a much sharper picture than if just natural arena-light was used.

Previous page: *The best photo of the best player in hockey history. This amazing Bob Mummery photo was reproduced in a 1000-copy limited edition run to commemorate Wayne Gretzky's record-setting 500 goals in 575 games. Note the surprised look on the referee's face as he watches Gretzky—flat out on a Quebec player's back—getting ready to shoot.*

BOB MUMMERY

Right: *Bob Mummery captures Dave Manson's elbow popping Brian MacLellan's helmet in 1989 playoff action. Is his head still in the helmet?*

CHRIS RELKE

On these pages, we've featured the work of two award-winning sports photographers—Bob Mummery and Chris Relke. Many other excellent photographers work around the NHL. The next time you look at a photo in a newspaper or magazine, look for the photographer's name in small print on the bottom right or left side of the picture. They help us in our enjoyment and understanding of the game.

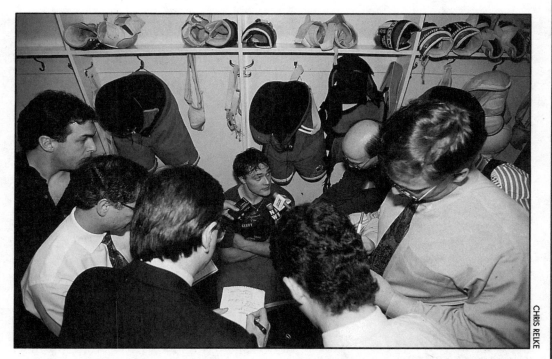

CHRIS RELKE

Above: *Sometimes an off-ice photo can be even more telling than a game-action one. Here, Relke shows us an exhausted Teemu Selanne who—after giving everything he could during the game—must still try to say something memorable for the media scrum.*

Previous page: *Chris Relke, a young Vancouver-based freelance photgrapher, captures Pavel Bure in mid-flight in these two photos taken a fraction of a second apart.*

The goalie has been called the last bastion of defense. Here, Bob Mummery shows us goalie Rick Wamsley protecting his net against the onrushing hordes.

BOB MUMMERY

Celebration! Those wondrous, sweet moments of victory that capture the essence of a game. Here, Mike Vernon enjoys a victory dance after another hard-fought win.

WHO AM I?

These drawings represent the last names of seven NHL players. We've given you a few hints for their first names. Can you guess who they are?

1

F _ _ I _ _ _ _ _ _ _ _ _ _ _ _

2

_ E _ _ Y _ _ _ _ _ _ _ _ _ _

3

_ _ C _ _ _ _ _ _ _ _

4

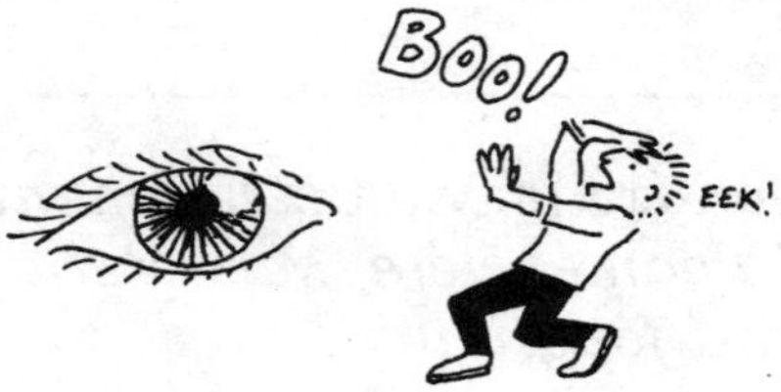

_ L _ _ _ _ _ _ _

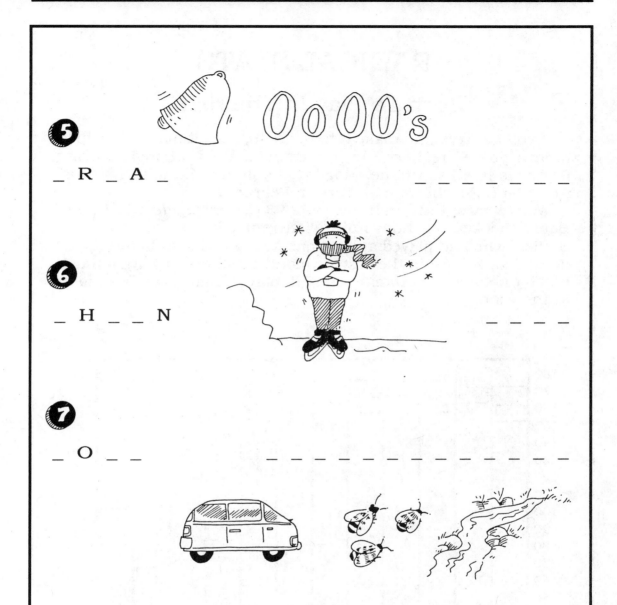

5 *OoOO's*

_ R _ A _   _ _ _ _ _ _ _

6

_ H _ _ N   _ _ _ _ _

7

_ O _ _   _ _ _ _ _ _ _ _ _

RADICAL STATS

Born To Play In The NHL?

If you are trying to make it to the NHL, does it matter in which month you were born? Is it a coincidence that high-scoring forwards like Lafontaine, Mogilny, Robitaille, Sundin, Lindros, Nolan and Recchi were all born in February?

Well, we went through the *1992-93 Official Guide and Record Book*, checked birthdays of all current players (not counting goalies) who had played at least one NHL game, and found that it does! People born in the first six months of the year have a much greater chance of becoming an NHL player than those born later in the year.

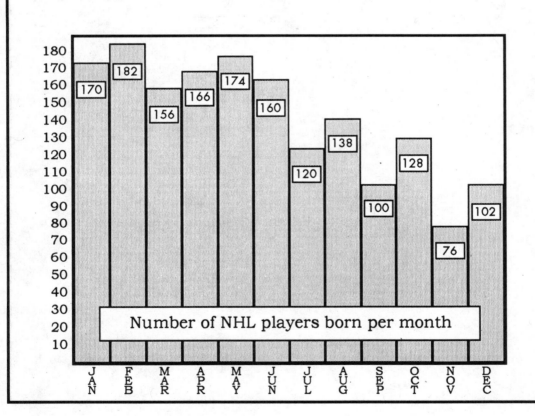

Number of NHL players born per month

JAN 170 | FEB 182 | MAR 156 | APR 166 | MAY 174 | JUN 160 | JUL 120 | AUG 138 | SEP 100 | OCT 128 | NOV 76 | DEC 102

RADICAL STATS

The graph on page 20 shows that February has 182 players, while November has only 76. In total, 1,008 players were born in the first six months with only 664 in the last six. We think it has something to do with age cut-offs for minor hockey. When you are six or seven years old, being eight or ten months older than the kids you play against can make a big difference.

Of course, there are exceptions to every rule: being born in August didn't stop Brett Hull, Pierre Turgeon or Adam Oates; September was good for Guy Lafleur and Bobby Orr; October was just fine for Mario Lemieux, while Sergei Fedorov and Ray Bourque have proven that, even if you're born in December, you can still make it to the NHL.

Born To Fight?

We noticed some players with tough-sounding last names, and wondered if they played tough as well. Over the years, the NHL has seen some pretty rough players. But do the players with tough-*sounding* names play tough on the ice?

Sometimes they do. For instance, Ronnie Stern averages over 250 penalty minutes per year in Calgary, while St. Louis Blues' Garth Butcher averages more than 200. And Lindy Ruff played tough for the Sabres and the Rangers during the 1980s.

Sometimes, though, names don't tell the story. Darren Rumble is a relatively mild-mannered defenseman for Ottawa, while now-retired Larry Playfair, averaging more than 150 penalty minutes per season, didn't always play fair.

Our all-time tough name dream team would consist of Ted Bulley (who played from 1976-'77 to 1983-'84), Spencer Meany (a Buffalo 1991 draft pick), and Reggie Savage (a 1988 Washington pick) as forwards; Garth Butcher and Darren Rumble on defense, and Jamie Ram (a Rangers' 1991 pick) in goal.

STANGEST LINE COMBINATIONS

In the early days, when the NHL was small enough for all the fans to know all the players, popular line combinations were often given nicknames. Two famous ones were The Production Line and The Kid Line. In the 1970s, Buffalo had the French Connection, with Gilbert Perreault centering Richard Martin and Rene Robert.

Russian hockey had the famous KLM line, with Vladimir **K**rutov, Igor **L**arionov and Sergei **M**akarov. Well, with a slight variation, the KLM line could fly again in San Jose, as first-round draft pick Viktor **K**ozlov could play with new Shark Igor **L**arionov and Sergei **M**akarov in 1993-'94.

But some wonderful line combinations could be created, if certain trades were made. What if Mark Lamb centered Jari Kurri and Steven Rice—would they be The Food Line? And with Bob Beers and Paul Coffey on defense, would the headlines read *Food & Drink = Success at Rink*?

But seriously, imagine the trouble announcers would get into if Mike Ricci, Mark Recchi and Joe Reekie were all on the ice at the same time. "Ricci, over to Recchi, back to Reekie, shoots, ooooh—tipped just wide by Ricci, trapped in the corner by Recchi, shovels it to Ricci, over to Reekie, back to Recchi, SCORES! Recchi from Reekie and Ricci."

Or how about the Colour Line, with Travis Green between Rob Brown and Sean Whyte? The Chuck Line, with Dale Hawerchuk centering Dave Andreychuk and Keith Tkachuk? The Ski Line, with Valeri Kamensky between Mike Krushelnyski and Bob Kudelski? Or even Team Brown—Doug, David and Rob Brown as forwards, with Keith and Jeff Brown on defense. Now, if they could only get former NHL goalies Andy or Ken Brown to come out of retirement and play nets, they'd have a complete team.

LONGEST NAMES

Have you ever wondered how many letters can be squeezed on the back of a hockey jersey? Probably not, but if you were an equipment manager it could be quite a problem, especially if Lou Franceschetti or Mike Krushelnyski were on your team.

For some reason, many current goalies have the longest names in the NHL today. John Vanbiesbrouck, at 13 letters, is the longest. Then comes Peter Sidorkiewicz with 12, Frank Pietrangelo and Mark Fitzpatrick at 11, and Stephane Beauregard, Craig Billington and Tommy Soderstrom at 10.

The longest name we found was John Brackenborough, whose 14 letters emblazoned the back of a Bruins jersey for only seven games in the 1949—'50season, and Steven Wojciechowski, who played for Detroit for two years in the mid-'40s.

CHRIS RELKE

RADICAL STATS

The Stanley Cup—Best Winning Records

We all know the Montreal Canadiens have won a ton of Stanley Cups. But which team, on average, wins them most often? To figure out which team has the best cup-winning percenage, we divided the number of cups they've won since the 1917-'18 season with the number of years they've been in the league. For instance, since the Penguins started in Pittsburgh in the 1967-'68 season, they've won the cup twice, so their average is once every 13 years, for an 8% Cup-winning percentage.

Note: these results were figured out at the end of the 1992-'93 season. We didn't include teams like the Victoria Cougars or Montreal Maroons that are no longer in the NHL, or the Ottawa Senators who have just returned after more than 60 years without an NHL team.

Team	Cups Won	Years in NHL	Average	Winning %
Montreal Canadiens	23 Cups	76 years	once every 3.3 years	30%
Toronto Maple Leafs	13 Cups	76 years	once every 5.8 years	17%
Detroit Red Wings	7 Cups	67 years	once every 9.6 years	10%
Edmonton Oilers	5 Cups	14 years	once every 2.8 years	36%
Boston Bruins	5 Cups	69 years	once every 13.8 years	7%
New York Islanders	4 Cups	21 years	once every 5.3 years	19%
Chicago Blackhawks	3 Cups	67 years	once every 22.3 years	4%
New York Rangers	3 Cups	67 years	once every 22.3 years	4%
Philadelphia Flyers	2 Cups	26 years	once every 13.0 years	8%
Pittsburgh Penguins	2 Cups	26 years	once every 13.0 years	8%
Calgary Flames	1 Cup	21 years	once every 21.0 years	5%

So, the Edmonton Oilers have a better Cup-winning percentage than Montreal!

RADICAL STATS

Is Bigger Better?

Eric Lindros is 6' 3", 235 pounds. Theoren Fleury is 5' 6", 160 pounds. Both are great players. And both are good examples of how, in hockey as well as in life, balance is important.

Hockey is a game of many parts. Team speed is as important as team size. When you look at almost every NHL team, you will now find a balance of both small and big forwards. Some of the NHL's biggest and smallest players are on the same team. In Vancouver, 5' 8" Cliff Ronning used to play centre between the twin peaks of 6' 3", 215-pound Sergio Momesso and 6' 3", 219-pound Jim Sandlak. Calgary has Fleury and 6' 4", 220 pound Joel Otto. Toronto has 6' 3", 225-pound Dave Andreychuk and 165-pound Doug Gilmour.

We thought it would be interesting to see if bigger is better, so we calculated the average team weight of forwards on the 1st and last team in each of the four 1992-'93 divisions.

In the Norris, Chicago finished first with 106 points while Tampa Bay had 53, exactly half. But the average weight of their forwards was exactly the same—190 pounds.

The Smythe had Vancouver in front with 101 points, more than four times the total of San Jose, who finished with only 24 points. Canucks forwards averaged 197 pounds, while the Sharks averaged 186.

Boston led the Adams with 109 points, poor Ottawa had only 24. But Boston's forwards averaged 188 pounds, six pounds less than Ottawa's 194 pound average.

And in the Patrick, the mighty Penguins had an incredible 119 points; the sixth place Rangers had 79. Pittsburgh median weight was 198, the Rangers 191.

Well, as far as we could tell, the forward lines on most teams average out about the same. Except, that is, for their skill levels!

THE FACES OF HOCKEY

Intense. Emotional. At times unmistakeable. The faces of hockey, as captured by sports photographers, give us an intimate glimpse into this fast-paced, exciting game.

Match the faces with the names of the players listed below.

Theoren Fleury
Doug Gilmour
Wayne Gretzky

Tim Hunter
Jaromir Jagr
Trevor Linden
Mark Messier

Mike Ricci
Jeremy Roenick
Teemu Selanne

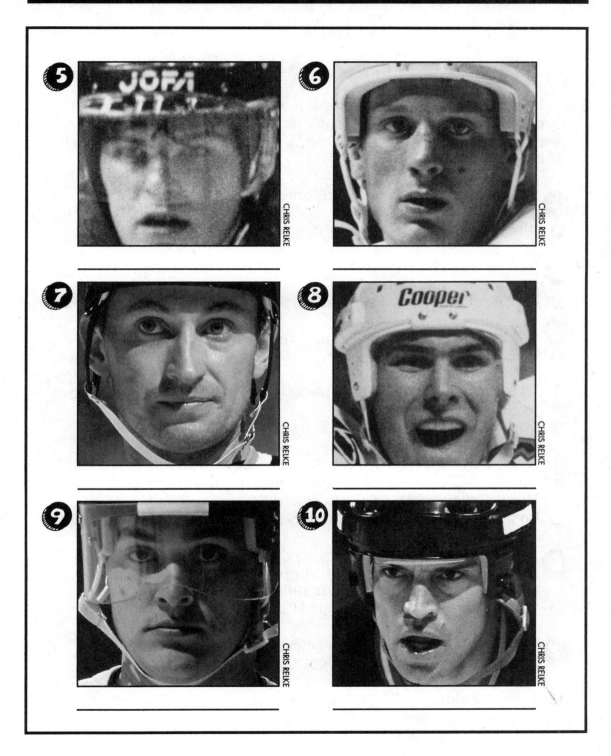

WHO SAID IT?

Hockey players are usually known for their actions, not their words. But sometimes they say some wonderful things, or others say memorable things about them. See if you can figure out who said what about whom!

1 "What I get paid for are the practices. I would play the games for nothing."
☑ Tim Horton ☐ Bobby Orr ☐ Eric Lindros

2 "I'm not a celebrity and I never will be. I go to the rink, do my job, and go home."
☐ Kirk Muller ☑ Paul Dipietro ☐ Guy Carbonneau

3 "I'd like to test myself against the best."
☐ Peter Forsberg ☑ Manon Rheaume ☐ Paul Kariya

4 "It's every boy's dream to play in the NHL, and I'm living out my dream."
☑ Luc Robitaille ☐ Nikolai Borschevsky ☐ Pat Burns

5 After Wayne Gretzky deflected a puck into his own net during the '93 Stanley Cup finals, which announcer said, "Even Betty Crocker burns a few cakes."?
☐ Foster Hewitt ☑ Harry Neale ☐ Jim Hughson

6 A former Soviet coach once said, "He is like an invisible man. He appears out of nowhere, passes to nowhere, and a goal is scored." Who was he talking about?
☐ Pavel Bure ☐ Brett Hull ☑ Wayne Gretzky

7 Who was Glen Williamson refering to when he said, "He's just unbelievable. He has got turbo-speed—Porsche speed."?
☑ Teemu Selanne ☐ Mike Gartner ☐ Trevor Linden

50-GOAL SCORERS

Scoring 50 goals in 50 games has always been considered the ultimate goal-scorer's feat. Since Montreal's Rocket Richard first accomplished this in the 1944-'45 season, only five different players have done it, though Wayne Gretzky has done it three times, and Brett Hull twice. Membership in this exclusive club only counts if the 50 goals were scored in the team's first 50 games.

A few more players have scored personal 50/50s. Alexander Mogilny scored 50 goals in his first 46 games during the 1992-'93 season, but his team had played 53 games. Likewise, Jari Kurri also has a personal, but not a team, 50 in 50.

While the old record for total 50-goal scorers during a season was ten in 1981-'82, usually only five to seven players per seaon reach the 50-goal mark. But during the 1992-'93 season, perhaps because of the weaker expansion teams and the addition of four more games to the season, this record was shattered—14 players scored 50 or more goals.

Test your knowledge about these players who have reached the 50-goal mark:

1 Who was the youngest player to score 50 goals?
❑ Teemu Selanne ❑ Jimmy Carson ❑ Wayne Gretzky

2 Who has scored the most 50-goal seasons in a row?
❑ Mike Bossy ❑ Mario Lemieux ❑ Wayne Gretzky

3 Which of these players has had a 50-goal season?
❑ Gordie Howe ❑ Hakan Loob ❑ Henri Richard

4 Which one of these players isn't a 50-goal scorer?
❑ Doug Gilmour ❑ Theoren Fleury ❑ Gary Roberts

PUZZLING PICTURES

See if you can figure out what these pictures represent. They are the names of current NHL coaches, teams or players, and one old-timer.

1 __ _ ___ __ __ _ __ __

2 _ _ _ _ __ _ _ _ _ _

3 _ _ _ _ _ __ _ _ _ _

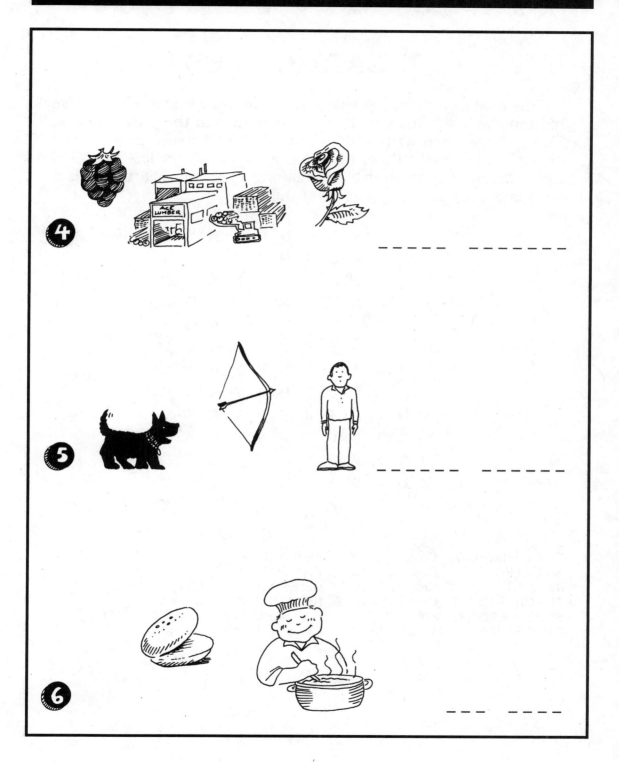

4. _ _ _ _ _ _ _ _ _ _ _ _

5. _ _ _ _ _ _ _ _ _ _ _ _

6. _ _ _ _ _ _ _ _

GREAT GOALIES

This goalie game might be the trickiest word search ever! We've hidden the last names of 23 current goalies in the puzzle below. Their names are written forwards or backwards, and placed horizontally, vertically or diagonally. The left-over letters (39 of them) taken in order from top to bottom, spell out the first and last names of four great goalies from the past.

```
V K E C N D R G P Y H Y E
B A R R A S S O D E E E A
H N N G L S T O E D X T D
E N B B N V E M H U T E L
A T E S I F A Y L R A G E
L U L N L E T U R H L G V
Y I F K J O S E P H L E E
N L O B R O D B A T E R H
O R U T E R R E R I R W C
N Y R A N F O R D O S A R
R H U F W W E E K S U C O
E H U K W A M S L E Y C Y
V M C L E A N A P P U P K
```

Tom BARRASSO	Glenn HEALY	Andy MOOG	John VANBIESBROUK
Ed BELFOUR	Ron HEXTALL	Felix POTVIN	Mike VERNON
Jon CASEY	Kelly HRUDEY	Daren PUPPA	Rick WAMSLEY
Tim CHEVELDAE	Curtis JOSEPH	Bill RANFORD	Steve WEEKS
Stephane FISET	Mike LIUT	Patrick ROY	Ken WREGGET
Grant FUHR	Kirk MCLEAN	Chris TERRERI	

_ _ _   _ _ _ _ _ _   ★   _ _ _ _ _   _ _ _ _

_ _ _ _   _ _ _ _ _ _   ★   _ _ _ _ _   _ _ _ _ _ _

AMAZING RECORDS

We'll be amazed if you know all of these NHL records.

1 Alexander Mogilny scored a goal only five seconds into a December 21, 1991 game between Buffalo and Toronto. He shares the 'fastest goal from the start of the game' record with two other players. Who are they?
- ❑ Wayne Gretzky & Mario Lemieux
- ❑ Dale Hawerchuk & Tim Kerr
- ❑ Bryan Trottier & Doug Smail

2 Which player has scored the most goals for a first-year expansion team?
- ❑ Brian Bradley—*Tampa Bay Lightning*
- ❑ Gilbert Perrault—*Buffalo Sabres*
- ❑ Pat Falloon—*San Jose Sharks*

3 The Calder Trophy is given each year to the NHL Rookie of the Year. Which one of these players has won the Calder?
- ❑ Gordie Howe ❑ Gary Suter ❑ Brett Hull

4 During the 1975 Stanley Cup finals between the Sabres and the Flyers, it was so hot in the Buffalo arena that dense fog formed above the ice. How many times did they have to stop the game in order to clear the fog?
- ❑ 11 ❑ 2 ❑ 19

5 The youngest player to ever play in the NHL was Bep Guidolin, who played for nine years starting in 1942-'43. How old was he?
- ❑ 14 ❑ 17 ❑ 16

6 Who was the first player on an expansion team (from 1968 onwards) to win the Hart Trophy as league MVP?
- ❑ Bobby Clarke ❑ Bryan Trottier ❑ Gilbert Perrault

PUZZLING LETTERS

Every sport has its common abbreviations. Baseball has RBIs and ERAs; football has QBs and TDs. Below we've combined some hockey abbreviations with common hockey phrases. For instance, 20 M in a P is 20 Minutes in a Period; 26 T in the NHL is, of course, 26 Teams in the NHL. Think you've got the hang of it?

1   3 P in a G = _____

2   3 G in a HT= _____

3   84 G in a S = _____

4   60 M in a G = _____

5   5 M in OT = _____

6   1 P on the I = _____

7   3 P on a FL = _____

8   2 G on the I = _____

9   50 G in 50 G = _____

10   1 R and 2 L per G = _____

11   7 G in a PS = _____

12   2 M in a MP = _____

13   10 M in a GM = _____

WHO IS THIS MAN?

And Why Is He Wearing A Calgary Flames Jersey?

Yes, you're right. It is Brett Hull, and he used to play for the Flames. In fact, he was drafted by them in 1984—117th overall! Hull, who played Junior B hockey in Penticton and then went to play college hockey in Minnesota, saw his first NHL action with the Flames in the 1985-'86 playoffs. The next year he played on their

minor league team in Moncton, New Brunswick, plus played five regular season and four playoff games for Calgary.

It wasn't until 1987-'88 that he broke into the NHL to stay, scoring 26 goals and getting 24 assists in 52 games for Calgary—and then they traded him! Along with Steve Bozek, he was traded to St. Louis for Rob Ramage and Rick Wamsley. And St. Louis has been happy ever since. By the end of the 1992-'93 season, in 402 games with the Blues, Brett Hull had scored an amazing 329 goals.

BOB MUMMERY

FACT OR FICTION?

In sports, as well as in life, it's sometimes hard to tell what's true and what isn't. In the questions below, see if you can spot the one *lie* buried in the three truths!

1 Pavel Bure, the exciting Vancouver Canuck who was Rookie of the Year for the 1991-'92 season:
- ❑ is usually among the top three NHLers in total shots on goal.
- ❑ broke the Canucks record for most goals by a rookie.
- ❑ won an Olympic gold medal for hockey.
- ❑ played on the same team as Sergei Fedorov and Alexander Mogilny.

2 The WHA (World Hockey Association), a rival league which ran from 1972-'73 to 1978-'79:
- ❑ was where four current NHL teams—Edmonton, Quebec, Hartford and Winnipeg—first started playing.
- ❑ had a team that was in such financial trouble that coach Harry Neale once gave out his team's wages in cash from a big brown paper bag.
- ❑ made Brett Hull's dad, Bobby Hull, the first million dollar hockey player.
- ❑ had an international division with regular league games in Sweden, Italy, Switzerland, and Germany.

3 The Quebec Nordiques, who started playing in the NHL during the 1979-'80 season:

❑ set an NHL record during 1992-'93 by improving 52 points over their previous season.

❑ have installed translation speakers in the helmets of English-speaking players, so they can understand their French-speaking coach.

❑ once played so poorly that angry fans littered the ice with rolls of toilet paper.

❑ one season won only two of   40 road games.

4 Coaches often have some interesting ideas, and do some fascinating things. At one time:

❑ Red Kelly, when coaching the Red Wings, made his players stand in the dressing room before a game under a giant pyramid, thinking it would bring them luck and strength.

❑ Scotty Bowman, who led the Canadiens to four straight Cup wins (1976 –'79) before winning one with Pittsburgh, used to keep his terrier named Scotty behind the bench with him.

❑ during the 1928 Stanley Cup playoffs, 44-year-old Ranger coach Lester Patrick was forced to play goal after his goalie was injured, and allowed only one goal in 18 shots.

❑ Roger Neilson, when coaching in junior hockey, used to take out his goalie and use a defenseman in net on penalty shots.

5 Which of the following NHL facts isn't true?

❑ Mike Gartner is the first player to score 30 or more goals in 14 straight seasons.

❑ Jeff Reese, a goalie for the Calgary Flames, once got an NHL-record three assists in one game.

❑ In his first-ever NHL game, Sandy Stevenson, a forward with the expansion California Seals, scored a hat trick against the Canadiens in the Montreal Forum.

❑ During a 13 – 1 victory over San Jose, the Calgary Flames got a record 3 goals in 53 seconds at the start of a period.

6 Some people say that goalies have the hardest job in the NHL—maybe that's why they have a reputation for doing some pretty odd things. For instance:

❑ Jacques Plante, the Hall of Fame goalie, used to knit wool hats to relax.

❑ famous Chicago and St. Louis Blues goalie Glenn Hall, who once described goaltending as "sixty minutes of hell," was so nervous before games that he would often throw up.

❑ Ron Hextall, who has a reputation for knowing how to use his stick on opposing players, is such a good fencer that he almost made the Canadian Olympic team.

❑ Gerry Cheevers, who played for 13 seasons, had a mask covered with black stitches that showed the number of times he'd been hit in the face.

7 Getting traded is a common NHL occurance, but some trades seem pretty weird. Did you know that:

❑ in 1978, during a poker game between general managers, Guy Lafleur was traded to the Red Wings, but the league commissioner vetoed the deal.

❑ one of the longest trades in NHL history was finally completed when the Oilers picked Nick Studuhar in the 1993 draft. Staduhar was 13 when Gretzky was traded to the Kings.

❑ a WHL player was once traded for a team bus.

❑ Brent Ashton started in the NHL during the 1979-'80 season. Since then he has played for nine different NHL teams.

8 Wayne Gretzky, holder of more hockey records than anyone in hockey history:
- ❑ received the Edmonton Oilers' first-ever NHL penalty, for slashing.
- ❑ was the Oilers' first captain in the NHL.
- ❑ started his pro career in Indianapolis.
- ❑ has a brother who was drafted by Tampa Bay Lightning.

9 Some pretty strange things can sometimes happen on the ice. Once during a game:
- ❑ a minor league linesman—who used to be a star New York Rangers defenseman—bodychecked a player who was going in on a breakaway.
- ❑ a little-used player got hungry warming the bench during an NHL game so he got an usher to bring him a hot dog. Shortly after, he was sent out to kill a penalty, crammed the dog into his glove, was checked and the hot dog squirted onto the ice.
- ❑ at the Forum in Los Angeles, a fan was once arrested for throwing a live chicken onto the ice.
- ❑ during the 1988 exhibition season, a game between the Leafs and Rangers was delayed because so many pucks were deflected into the stands that they ran out and had to buy more from the souvenir stand in the rink.

THE CALDER TROPHY

Each year, the Calder Trophy—named after a former NHL president—is given to the top rookie in the NHL. It's chosen by the Professional Hockey Writer's Association, and was first given out in 1933.

What amazed us was the number of excellent hockey players—high-scorers like Luc Robitaille, Dale Hawerchuk, and Joe Nieuwendyk—who win the Calder, then never win another individual trophy for the rest of their careers.

Obviously, only one player can win the Hart Trophy as the league MVP; only one defenseman win the Norris; one goalie the Vezina (best goalie); one sniper the Art Ross Trophy for scoring; one playoff hero the Smythe. As well, there is the Masterton Trophy for perseverance, and the Pearson for best player, chosen by the players themselves.

On the next page is a list of the Calder Trophy winners from the last 20 years, plus other trophies they've won.

BOB MUMMERY

Can you guess this Calder Trophy winner?

CALDER TROPHY WINNERS

1974 — Denis Potvin
  3 Norris
1975 — Eric Vail
1976 — Bryan Trottier
  1 Ross, 1 Hart,
  1 Smythe, 1 Clancy
1977 — Willi Plett
1978 — Mike Bossy
  1 Smythe
1979 — Bobby Smith
1980 — Ray Bourque
  4 Norris, 1 Clancy
1981 — Peter Stastny
1982 — Dale Hawerchuk
1983 — Steve Larmer

1984 — Tom Barrasso
1985 — Mario Lemieux
  4 Ross, 2 Hart,
  3 Pearson, 2 Smythe
  1 Masterton
1986 — Gary Suter
1987 — Luc Robitaille
1988 — Joe Nieuwendyk
1989 — Brian Leetch
  1 Norris
1990 — Sergei Makarov
1991 — Ed Belfour
  2 Vezina, 2 Jennings
1992 — Pavel Bure
1993 — Teemu Selanne

UP FRONT

Can you identify each of the players pictured on the front cover?

Los Angeles King (#99) = _____

Vancouver Canuck (#10) = _____

Chicago Blackhawk (#30) = _____

Montreal Canadien (#11) = _____

Buffalo Sabre (#89) = _____

MARIO THE MAGNIFICENT

Generally agreed to be the best player in hockey today, Lemieux has risen to the top even though he hasn't played a full season since the 1988-'89 season. In the four years following, chronic back problems kept him out an average of 29 games a year; his highest total was 64 games.

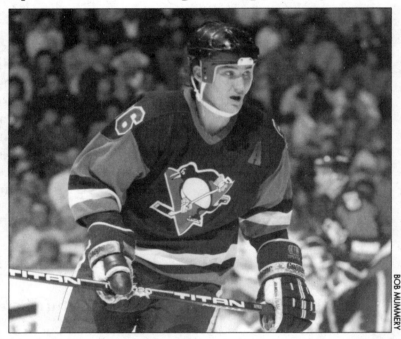

And yet, four times in the last six years he led the league in scor-ing, twice won the Hart as league MVP, twice won the Smythe as playoff MVP, and helped the Penguins win two Cups.

But his big-gest challenge came in Janu-ary of '93 when he was diagnosed with Hodgkin's disease, a form of cancer. At the time, he had a huge lead in the scoring race. With Mario out of the lineup, the Penguins struggled to play .500 hockey. After taking time off for surgery, radiation treatment, and rest, he returned and continued scoring at a record pace. Playing only 60 out of 84 games, he still scored 69 goals and 91 assists for 160 points to win another scoring title. If he had played a full season, those 160 points would have translated into 224 points.

Recurring back problems also kept him out for the start of the 1993-'94 season. Let's hope he's healthy enough to play a full season soon.

COLLECTIBLES

Top Ten Draft Picks—& Their Rookie Cards

In hockey, there are good draft years, and bad ones. Some years, like 1990, are extremely strong. Nine of the top ten picks—including stars like Jaromir Jagr, Mike Ricci, and Owen Nolan—have played in the NHL. While other years, like in 1989, only #1 overall Mats Sundin has made an impact.

Sometimes a single player—like 1991's Eric Lindros or 1993's Alexandre Daigle—eclipse the rest of the draft. And so it goes—one or two impact NHLers out of the top ten chosen. When you consider the number of players drafted each year—more than 260—you see how difficult it is to actually make it to the NHL.

The same is true for hockey card collectors—knowing that only a handful of the huge number of players with rookie cards each year will ever play in the NHL, it's hard to know who to collect.

We thought it would be interesting to check the card values of top draft choices over the years, so we priced the first ten picks from 1979 to 1988. What we found was, on average, one or two players per year whose cards had real value. Some years there were solid gold rookie cards—like 1984 #1 draft pick Mario Lemieux, whose OPC rookie card is now worth more than $400. Or Ray Bourque in 1979 (around $150), Paul Coffey in 1980 (approximately $120), or Steve Yzerman in '83 (approximately $60). Other years, like 1985, it's only pack after pack of commons—Wendel Clark's rookie card, at around $7, is the highest card of the top ten. But like it sometimes takes time for a player to mature, it also takes time for cards to rise. Collecting top ten picks might help keep you interested in a player's career for many years.

Some people collect goalies or specialize in players on a certain team. Others collect players from their home-town, or province or state. A few focus on players that were low draft choices but who the collector thinks will become future stars. They study their early stats and keep a close eye on minor leagues results, hoping their players will be called up. There are sometimes gems in early commons, when genuine stars rise from the depths of their draft position—Brett Hull was chosen 117th overall, and Theoren Fleury 166th.

One collector we know wants to visit Scandinavia, so he's been collecting commons and cheap cards of all the Swedish and Finnish players he can find. He's got hundreds of Jari Kurri, Esa Tikkanen, Thomas Sandstrom, and Mats Sundin cards, as well as some early cards of the first European NHL players like Borje Salming and Kent Nilsson. Hockey cards are easy to carry on a trip as they don't take up much room, and he hopes to sell them and make some spending money when he's there.

Thommie Bergman's Rookie Card, OPC, 1973. Bergman, a Swedish defenseman who played in the NHL from 1972-'73 to 1979-'80, was the first European-born player to ever play for Detroit.

Obviously, there are many different ways to collect cards. Erwin Borau, the owner of an excellent card shop in Penticton, B.C., advises young collectors to "start by collecting their favourite players and teams. Most of the top players have many cards produced each year and it can be both challenging and fun trying to get one of each card." He feels that the hockey card market will continue for many years, though with fewer dealers and manufacturers overall.

One thing, of course, to remember about cards if you're selling them—just because it's listed in a price guide at a certain price, don't expect to get the full price listed. Many dealers, and they have to *want* the card in the first place, will only pay a quarter or a third of the price listed. Better to trade with friends or other collectors, or get a table at a flea market or inexpensive card show and wait until someone really wants what you've got to sell.

Many hockey players also collect cards. It's been written that Patrick Roy has an incredible hockey card collection, many of them autographed by current and past greats. With the high price of both cards and NHL salaries, maybe hockey players are the only people able to buy all the cards they want!

ANSWERS

Nicknames—page 6
Pavel Bure—*Russian Rocket*
Bobby Hull—*Golden Jet*
Brett Hull—*Golden Brett*
Al Iafrate—*Wild Thing*
Darius Kasparaitis—*Lethal Lithuanian*
Ted Kennedy—*Teeder*
Mario Lemieux—*Super Mario*
Eric Lindros—*The Next One*
Kirk McLean—*Captain Kirk*
Alexander Mogilny—*Alexander The Great*
Mark Recchi—*Rex*
Vladimir Ruzicka—*Rosie*
Jim Sandlak—*House*
Teemu Selanne—*Finnish Flash*
Bryan Trottier—*Trots*
George Vezina—*Chicoutimi Cucumber*
Lorne Worsley—*Gump*
Zarley Zalapski—*Double Z*
Valeri Zelepukin—*Pukie*

Where Were They Born—page 7
Pavel Bure—*Russia*
Doug Gilmour—*Canada*
Brian Glynn—*Germany*
Mark Hardy—*Switzerland*
Jaromir Jagr—*Czechoslovakia*
Brian Leetch—*United States*
Jyrki Lumme—*Finland*
Owen Nolan—*Northern Ireland*
Jim Paek— *South Korea*
Steve Smith—*Scotland*
Mats Sundin—*Sweden*

Are You Kidding—page 8
1) his motorcycle fell on him.
2) Ray Ferraro
3) Peter Zezel
4) hit in the face with a whipped cream pie.
5) Wayne Gretzky
6) Stan Mikita
7) playing in a Las Vegas parking lot.

Who Am I—page 18
1) Felix Potvin
2) Kelly Buchberger
3) Luc Robitaille
4) Al Iafrate
5) Brian Bellows
6) Shawn Burr
7) John Vanbiesbrouck

The Faces of Hockey—page 26
1) Mike Ricci
2) Tim Hunter
3) Theoren Fleury
4) Doug Gilmour
5) Jaromir Jagr
6) Jeremy Roenick
7) Wayne Gretzky
8) Trevor Linden
9) Teemu Selanne
10) Mark Messier

Who Said It—page 28
1) Tim Horton
2) Paul Dipietro
3) Manon Rheaume
4) Luc Robitaille
5) Harry Neale
6) Wayne Gretzky
7) Teemu Selanne

50-Goal Scorers—page 29
1) Wayne Gretzky
2) Mike Bossy
3) Hakan Loob
4) Doug Gilmour

Puzzling Pictures—page 30
1) Los Angeles Kings
2) Adam Graves
3) Trent Yawney
4) Barry Melrose
5) Scotty Bowman
6) Bun Cook

ANSWERS

Fan Favourites—page 11
★ Lafleur
★ Howe
★ Richard
★ Esposito

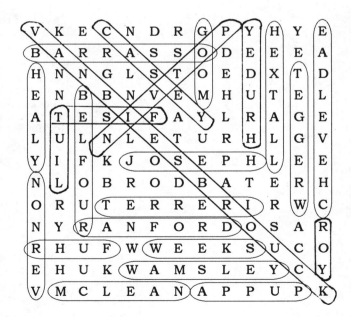

Great Goalies—page 32
★ Ken Dryden
★ Glenn Hall
★ Turk Broda
★ Terry Sawchuk

ANSWERS

Amazing Records—page 31
1) Bryan Trottier & Doug Smail
2) Brian Bradley
3) Gary Suter
4) 11
5) 16
6) Bobby Clarke

Puzzling Letters—page 32
1) 3 Periods in a Game
2) 3 Goals in a Hat Trick
3) 84 Games in a Season
4) 60 Minutes in a Game
5) 5 Minutes in Over-Time
6) 1 Puck on the Ice
7) 3 Players on a Forward Line
8) 2 Goalies on the Ice
9) 50 Goals in 50 Games
10) 1 Referee and 2 Linesmen per Game
11) 7 Games in a Playoff Series
12) 2 Minutes in a Minor Penalty
13) 10 Minutes in a Game Misconduct

Fact or Fiction—page 36
1) won an Olympic gold medal for hockey.
2) had an international division with regular league games in Sweden, Italy, Switzerland and Germany.
3) have installed translation speakers in the helmets of English-speaking players.
4) Scotty Bowman used to keep his terrier named Scotty behind the bench with him.
5) In his first-ever NHL game, Sandy Stevenson scored a hat trick against the Canadiens.
6) Ron Hextall is such a good fencer that he almost made the Olympic team.
7) in 1978, during a poker game between general managers, Guy Lafleur was traded to the Red Wings.
8) was the Oilers' first captain in the NHL.
9) During the 1988 exhibition season, a game between the Leafs and Rangers was delayed because so many pucks were deflected into the stands that they ran out.

Calder Trophy—page 40
Joe Nieuwendyk

Front cover photos—page 41
L.A. King = Wayne Gretzky
Vancouver Canuck = Pavel Bure
Chicago Blackhawk = Ed Belfour
Montreal Canadien = Kirk Muller
Buffalo Sabre = Alexander Mogilny